This book belongs to ♡ W9-BZX-624

Cheryl Ng

Draw a picture of yourself

Color in using beautiful colors!

Doodlepedia
Pretty

A WORLD of pretty DOODLES and FABULOUS FACTS

DK

LONDON, NEW YORK, MELBOURNE, MUNICH, AND DELHI

Edited by Alexander Cox, Lee Wilson
Designed by Jess Bentall, Anna Formanek,
Charlotte Johnson
Text by Alexander Cox, Wendy Horobin,
Susan Maylan, Ben Morgan, Lee Wilson
Fact checker Wendy Horobin
Illustrators Emma Atkinson, Holly Blackman,
Amber Cassidy, Helen Dodsworth, Evannave, Nic Farrell
US Editor Margaret Parrish
Managing Editor Penny Smith
Managing Art Editor Marianne Markham
Art director Jane Bull
Category publisher Mary Ling
Producer (Preproduction) George Nimmo
Senior Producer (Preproduction) Tony Phipps
Senior Production Controller Seyhan Esen
Creative Technical Support Sonia Charbonnier

First published in the United States in 2012 by
DK Publishing
375 Hudson Street, New York, New York 10014

Copyright© 2012 Dorling Kindersley Limited
12 13 14 15 16 10 9 8 7 6 5 4 3 2 1
001—186246—10/12

A catalog record for this book is available from the
Library of Congress.
ISBN: 978-0-7566-9799-0
Printed and bound in China by Leo Paper Products Ltd.

All images © Dorling Kindersley
For further information see: www.dkimages.com
Discover more at www.dk.com

FLATS OR SKY-HIGH HEELS?
DESIGN YOUR OWN SHOE.

DANCE WITH THE CHINESE DRAGON
AND COLOR HIM IN.

Doodlepedia

A WORLD of pretty DODDLES and FABULOUS FACTS

DRAW BABY TURTLES SCRAMBLING TO THE WATER.

CAN YOU FIND ALL OF THE OWLS?

GO DOODLING CRAZY IN THE EMPTY BOX.

DOODLEPEDIA is exactly what it says—a book of doodling! **COLOR, DESIGN,** and **DRAW** all over the pages and learn as you create. Find out about hummingbirds, henna, mazes, and lots more! Are you ready for oodles of doodling fun? Then turn the page and begin!

Can you **FIND** your way through the mystifying maze?

Lost in a hedgerow!

Have you ever tried to find your way around a **maze**? Mazes are **outdoor puzzles** formed by **high hedges**. There are two types of maze. **Branching mazes** have only one path to the center. **Island mazes** have several. Both are full of **forked paths** and **dead ends**, but you can always find your way to the center and out of a branched maze by keeping your right hand on the wall.

FIND YOUR WAY TO THE CENTER OF THE MAZE.

The **oldest** surviving hedge maze is in the gardens of **Hampton Court Palace** near London. It was built in 1690 for King William III and is still in use.

FINISH

START

Henna patterns!

Henna is a plant dye that has been used in the ancient art of tattooing for **thousands of years**. Unlike modern tattooing, which injects permanent inks into the skin, henna is a paste that **temporarily dyes** the outer layer of skin. Henna art can last for up to a month, depending on your skin type. Henna is mainly used to decorate hands, feet, and arms in **cultural ceremonies**, such as weddings. The artwork takes its influence from Southern Asia, Northern Australasia, and Africa, where henna originates.

Ground henna leaves form a powder.

DESIGN YOUR OWN HENNA TATTOOS ON THE HANDS AND FEET!

The palms of the hands and the soles of the feet are popular locations for henna tattoos because the skin is thick, which makes the henna art last longer.

DESIGN pretty henna patterns or makeup.

The peacock's **train** is not its tail, but is actually a series of **long feathers** that spring up from its back.

COLOR IN THE PROUD PEACOCK.

Shake a tail feather!

Peafowl are large birds that originally came from Asia. The males of the blue peafowl are called **peacocks**. They have a vibrant bluey-green **plumage** and an elaborate **train of feathers** that they **fan out** to **attract** females. These feathers are **patterned** with "eyes" that **shimmer** in the light. Females are called **peahens** and are mainly brown and gray in color. When choosing a mate, the female counts the number of "eyes" in the male's train. The one with the most gets the girl!

An Albino peacock has an elaborate train, but it is **completely white**.

Behind the mask!

Every year in **Venice**, Italy, the residents hold a **carnival** where it is traditional to wear a **mask**. In the 13th century, masks were used to **hide** the wearer's **identity** and were worn for **romantic encounters** or for **political matters**. Carnival masks are often **highly decorated** and **adorned** with **jewels, ribbons,** and **feathers**.

Masks can cover the whole face (called a **Bauta**) or just the eyes (a **Columbina**).

DESIGN MORE BEAUTIFUL VENETIAN MASKS.

CREATE AND COLOR PATTERNS
FOR YOUR QUILT, USING TRIANGLES, SQUARES, AND HEXAGONS.

Crazy patchwork!

Patchwork is **sewing** two or more pieces of material together—it's like making a fabric sandwich! Pieces of **fabric** are stitched together into **patterns**, then **sewn** to a layer of padded filling. Quilting is an **ancient art**. A 5,500-year-old **Egyptian** statue shows a Pharaoh in a quilted cloak, and in medieval times, Arab and European soldiers wore **quilted robes** under their metal armor. In China, **warm clothes** have been made of quilted cloth for centuries. It is also used around the world to make **bed spreads**, curtains, and decorative hangings.

Today, colorful quilts are often made as **gifts** and passed down within **families** from generation to generation.

Zany zebra stripes!

Just like snowflakes, no two **zebras** are alike—each one has a **unique pattern** of **black and white stripes**. Zebras look striking to human eyes, but their bold colors help them **hide from danger**. The stripes may also make herds of galloping zebras seem to **blur together**, confusing **lions** on the hunt.

Zebras are black, with white stripes on top. They **start out black** in their mother's womb and get **white stripes** as they develop.

DRAW STRIPES ON THE ZEBRAS.

DRAW MORE OBJECTS AND **FINISH** THE RAINBOW.

Rainbows actually form as a **full circle**. We only see them as an arc because the horizon blocks the remaining rainbow from our view.

Rainbows can occur at night.
This is called a **moonbow**! It's
rare to spot one, however,
since the **Moon** has to be bright
enough and in the right place
for you to see a moonbow.

Let there be light!

What color is **sunlight**? Yellow? Does it even have a color? Actually, sunlight is a **mixture of different colors**. We can see these colors in all their glory when it is **raining** but the **Sun** is still **shining**. As the sunlight **shines** through the raindrops, the **light bends**, revealing a range of colors in a beautiful arc in the sky—a **rainbow**!

It's snowing!

It's always exciting when snow starts to fall. These fluffy **snowflakes** started life as miniscule **crystals of ice**, high up in the clouds. The crystals gradually join together to make heavier six-sided **clusters** that start to fall toward the ground. If the **air temperature** is **cold** enough, the clusters fall to Earth as snowflakes.

COMPLETE THE FALLING SNOWFLAKES.

Snowflakes always have **six branches**, but they come in an endless **variety** of **patterns** and **sizes**. No two snowflakes are ever the same.

Most snowflakes are so **tiny** that we can only see their shapes through a **microscope**. The snow that arrives on the ground is usually groups of flakes clumped together.

Welcome to our watery world!

This water is beautiful! **Tropical fish** are from the **tropics**, so the **water temperature** in this type of **aquarium** needs to be around 80°F (27°C)—just as it would be in the warm tropics. Aquariums need a **filter** to keep the water **clean,** and a **light** to help the tank **plants** to grow. Be careful what fish you put in the tank though—some can be pretty **feisty** when they want to be...

DRAW MORE FISH SWIMMING.

Angelfish come from the **Amazon River** in South America. They get their name from their beautiful **fins**, which look like **angels' wings**.

That's fashion!

Do you keep up with the latest **trends** in **fashion**? Every year **designers** decide on the **hottest styles** and hold **fashion shows** to showcase their designs. Fashion has always been big—just look at old paintings to see what was once considered **fashionable**. Today, the **main centers** for fashion are **Paris**, **Milan**, **New York City**, and **London**, and each holds a huge show every year, showing off the best of fashion.

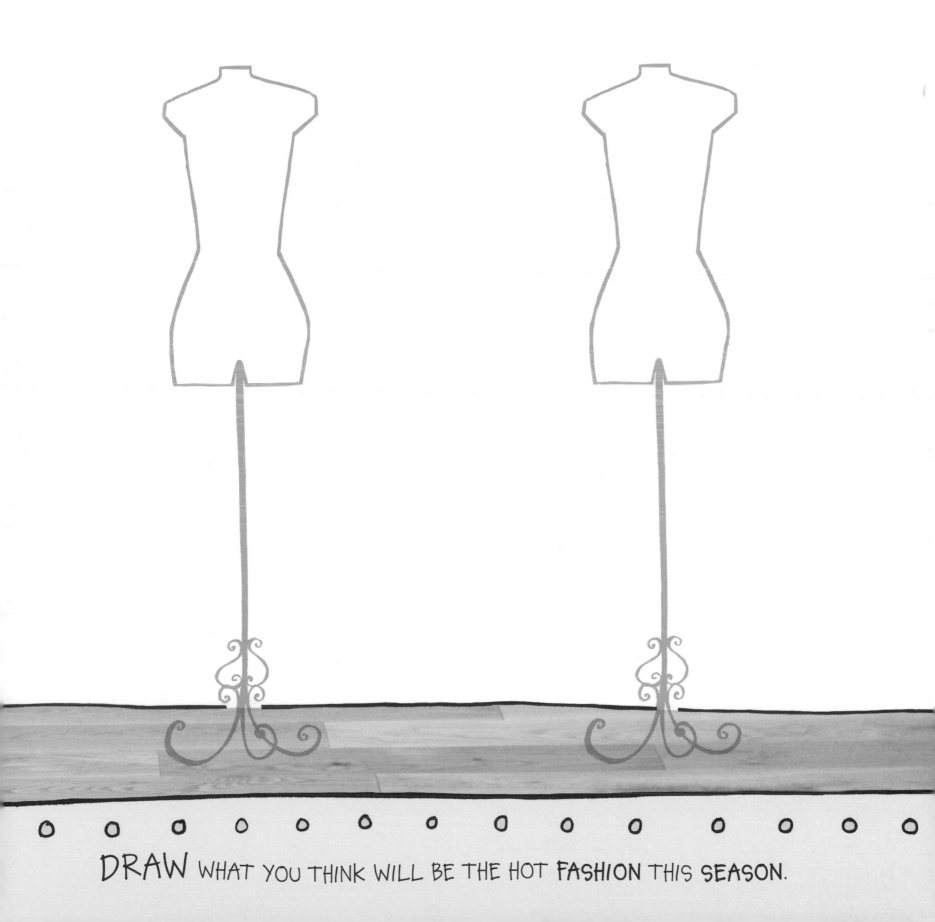

DRAW WHAT YOU THINK WILL BE THE HOT **FASHION** THIS **SEASON**.

When the cathedral was first built, it was painted **white with gold domes**. The patterns and colors we see today were **added** in the 19th century.

COLOR IN THE CATHEDRAL.

Many people think the **onion domes** represent **burning candles**, but no one really knows why many Russian churches have these domes.

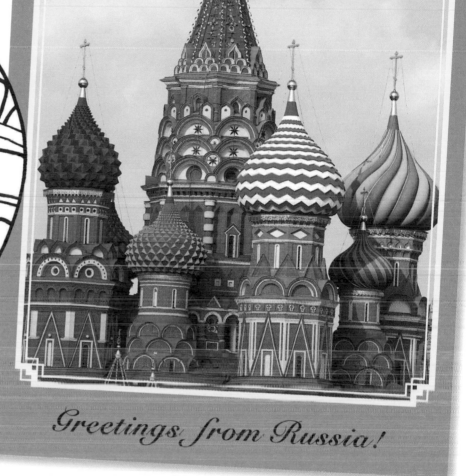

Greetings from Russia!

A czar and 10 onions!

This amazing building is **St. Basil's Cathedral**, which stands in the very center of **Moscow, Russia**. It consists of one big church and nine smaller ones each topped by a brightly painted, **onion-shaped dome**. It was built in 1555–60 for **Czar Ivan the Terrible**, who really was terrible! According to one legend, he had the architect of St. Basil's blinded so that he could not build anything more beautiful.

Sunny sunflowers!

Sunflowers are easy to grow. Plant the seeds in soil, provide some warmth, light, and water and they will become tall, leafy plants with **beautiful flowers**. However, what we think of as one flower is actually lots of tiny flowers, called **florets**, clustered together in a pattern of **spirals** and surrounded by a frill of yellow petals. Each of these flowers eventually produces a tasty **seed**, which is used to make cooking oil and vegetable oil spreads.

DRAW AND COLOR SOME BRIGHT SUNFLOWERS TO FILL THE POTS.

Some types of sunflower are **incredibly tall**. The record is 26 ft 4 in (8.04 m)—that's taller than four adults standing on top of each other!

Sunflowers **turn** their heads daily to follow the **Sun's path** across the sky.

Scramble to the sea!

When a **mother sea turtle** is ready to **lay her eggs**, she swims ashore, and lays and **buries her eggs in a hole** on a sandy beach. Once she's laid them all, she crawls back into the sea. After hatching, it may take the **baby turtles** three or more days to dig their way out of the nest, then it's a quick **nighttime scramble** down the beach and off to sea!

A baby turtle has a **small horn** on its head, called an **egg-tooth**, which it uses to break out of the egg.

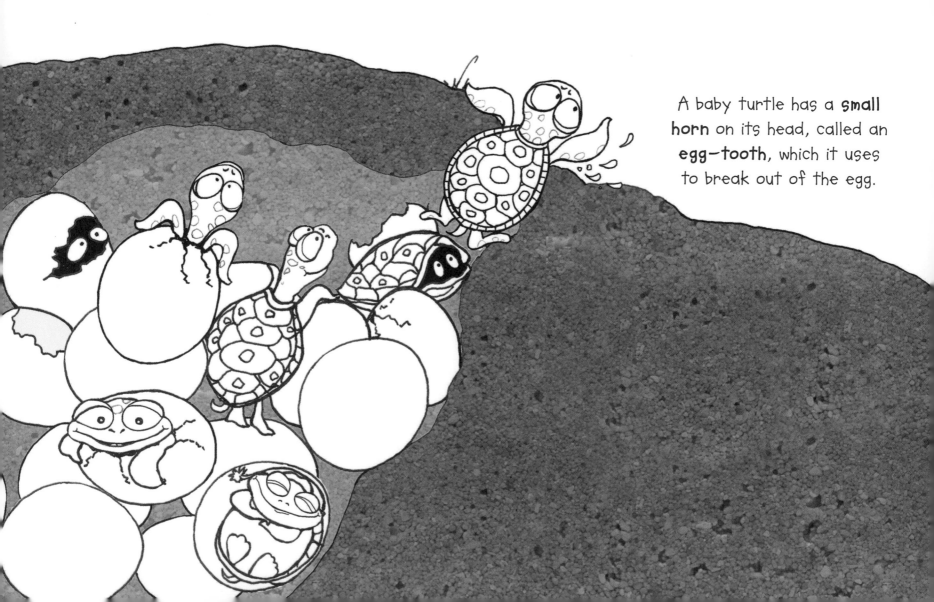

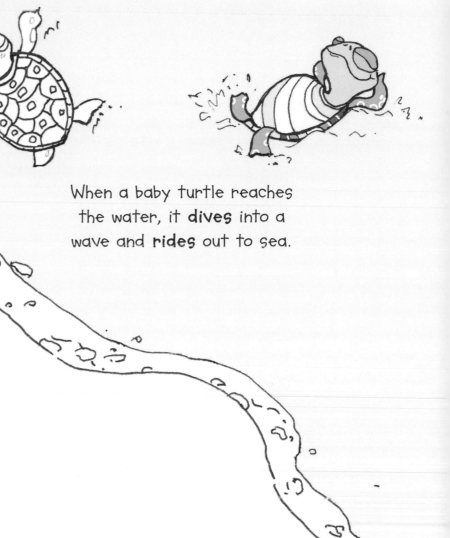

When a baby turtle reaches the water, it **dives** into a wave and **rides** out to sea.

DRAW MORE BABY TURTLES CRAWLING TO THE SEA.

Keep your hat on!

Why do people wear **hats**? There are many reasons—to keep their heads **warm**, for **safety**, to keep the rain or sun off, or as a **fashion accessory**. The first hats were **simple in shape** and made of **fabric** or **woven straw**. Modern hats can be **masterpieces** of creative sculpture, featuring elaborately **wild** and **wacky designs** made to grab attention.

The singer Lady Gaga has worn a variety of **strange hats**. She has a hat with a **telephone** attached, and even one with a **diamond-encrusted lobster** stuck on the front!

DRAW OUTRAGEOUS AND STYLISH HATS.

Amazing Amazon!

The **Amazon** is the largest **rainforest** in the world. It covers an amazing 2.3 million square miles (6 million square kilometers)—that's nearly twice as big as India! **Fifty percent of all known animal and plant species** on Earth live in this **hot, damp environment**, which has **four** distinct **habitats**: the dark **forest floor** (only 2% of light reaches this far down), the **understory**, the **canopy**, and finally the **emergent layer**, which is the top of the tallest trees.

COLOR THE GOLDEN LION TAMARIN MONKEYS YELLOW.

One of the most difficult jumps is the entrechat-douze, where the dancer has to **cross and uncross her legs six times** while **jumping** vertically.

On your toes!

Ballet is a dance style that began in Italy in the 15th century and spread to France and Russia, where it was developed into the **performance art** we know today. **Classical ballet** depends on a dancer learning how to perfect the steps, poses, and jumps. Every ballet dancer will learn the **five basic positions**. These are very important, since every basic move in ballet begins and ends with one of these positions.

DRAW MORE BALLERINAS DANCING.

1. Heels touching and feet pointing outward.

2. Feet pointing outward and heels apart.

3. One foot in front with the heel touching the middle of the back foot.

4. The feet are in the same place as for position 3, but one step apart.

5. Feet crossed so the toes of each foot touch the heels of the other.

COLOR THE TEMPLES AND DRAGONS.

This building is the **City Pillar shrine** in the town of **Suphan Buri, Thailand.** Like all Chinese-style **temples,** it has a **symmetrical** design, which symbolizes **balance** and **harmony.**

Greetings!

The two figures at the entrance to the **shrine** are **guardian lions,** known as "Shishi." They stand with one paw resting on a ball, which represents the **world.**

Dragons on the roof!

Perched high up on the roof of a **Thai temple,** these **dragons** may look scary, but they are actually **good-luck charms.** Dragons are quite common **decorations** on the roofs of **palaces, temples,** and other important Chinese buildings and represent **power, strength,** and **good fortune.** In Chinese myths, they are the **rulers of rivers and seas** and are in **charge of the rain.**

Look out!

Gangs of meerkats pop out of their underground burrows to search for food. But while some are foraging for insects, others are on sentry duty and stand up on their hind legs looking all around for any possible danger. If they spot a predator, they quickly raise the alarm by barking or whistling, and everyone dives down the nearest hole to safety.

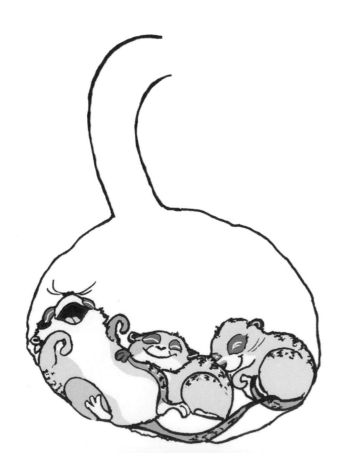

Meerkats live in underground burrows, which consist of tunnels and chambers where they sleep. There may be up to 70 different entrances to a burrow system.

COMPLETE THE PASSAGES SO THE MEERKATS CAN GET BACK TO THEIR CHAMBERS.

Meerkats are not cats at all—they are members of the **mongoose** family. They live in **southern Africa**, particularly the **Kalahari Desert**.

It's showtime!

People have been **performing** and **entertaining** in the theater for centuries. **Playwrights** may invent **stories** or they may try and create dramatic retellings of **historical events**. Some plays are pure entertainment, while others are performed to tell people about past events or to teach them about **good** and **evil**.

The **two masks** used as a traditional **symbol** for theater represent the Greek goddesses of **tragedy** (the sad face) and **comedy** (the happy face).

DESIGN THE SCENERY FOR YOUR PLAY.

COMPLETE THE SCENE WITH ACTORS.

No you're not imagining things, hummingbirds really can fly **upside down**! They can even fly **backwards**!

Hummingbirds!

You have heard of birds singing, but what about birds that hum? **Hummingbirds** get their name because they flap their wings so fast (up to 80 times a second) that they make a **humming** sound. They move their wings in a figure–eight pattern, which allows them to **hover** near a sweet–smelling flower. They can then lick the yummy **nectar** inside, or catch a tasty bug.

DRAW AND COLOR MORE HUMMINGBIRDS.

There are over three hundred species of hummingbird, including the **sparkling violet-eared hummingbird**. This colorful bird doesn't just hum, it also sings to declare its territory!

It's just a dream!

When you **sleep** you have dreams. But what are dreams? This question has been asked for a very long time and no one knows for sure, even though there are lots of different theories. Dreams **conjure up** images, people, and events that can be exciting, scary, and sometimes, really dull. Bad dreams are known as **nightmares** and can frighten you so you suddenly wake up. But don't worry—it's just a dream.

Some people only dream in **black and white!**

You only dream about **things you know.** So the strangers in your dreams are people you've seen in real life.

DRAW ONE OF YOUR OWN DREAMS.

Henna patterns!

Henna is a plant dye that has been used in the ancient art of tattooing for **thousands of years**. Unlike modern tattooing, which injects permanent inks into the skin, henna is a paste that **temporarily dyes** the outer layer of skin. Henna art can last for up to a month, depending on your skin type. Henna is mainly used to decorate hands, feet, and arms in **cultural ceremonies**, such as weddings. The artwork takes its influence from Southern Asia, Northern Australasia, and Africa, where henna originates.

Ground henna leaves form a powder.

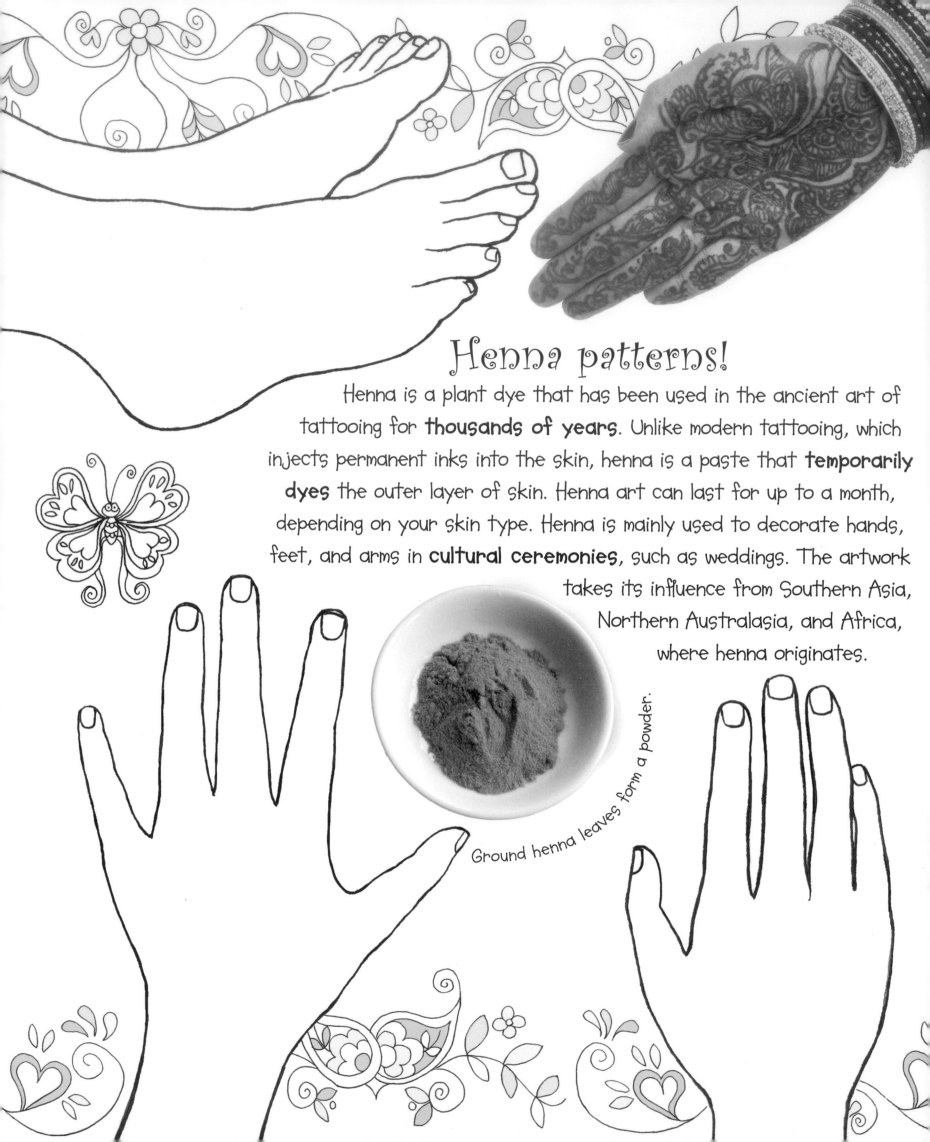

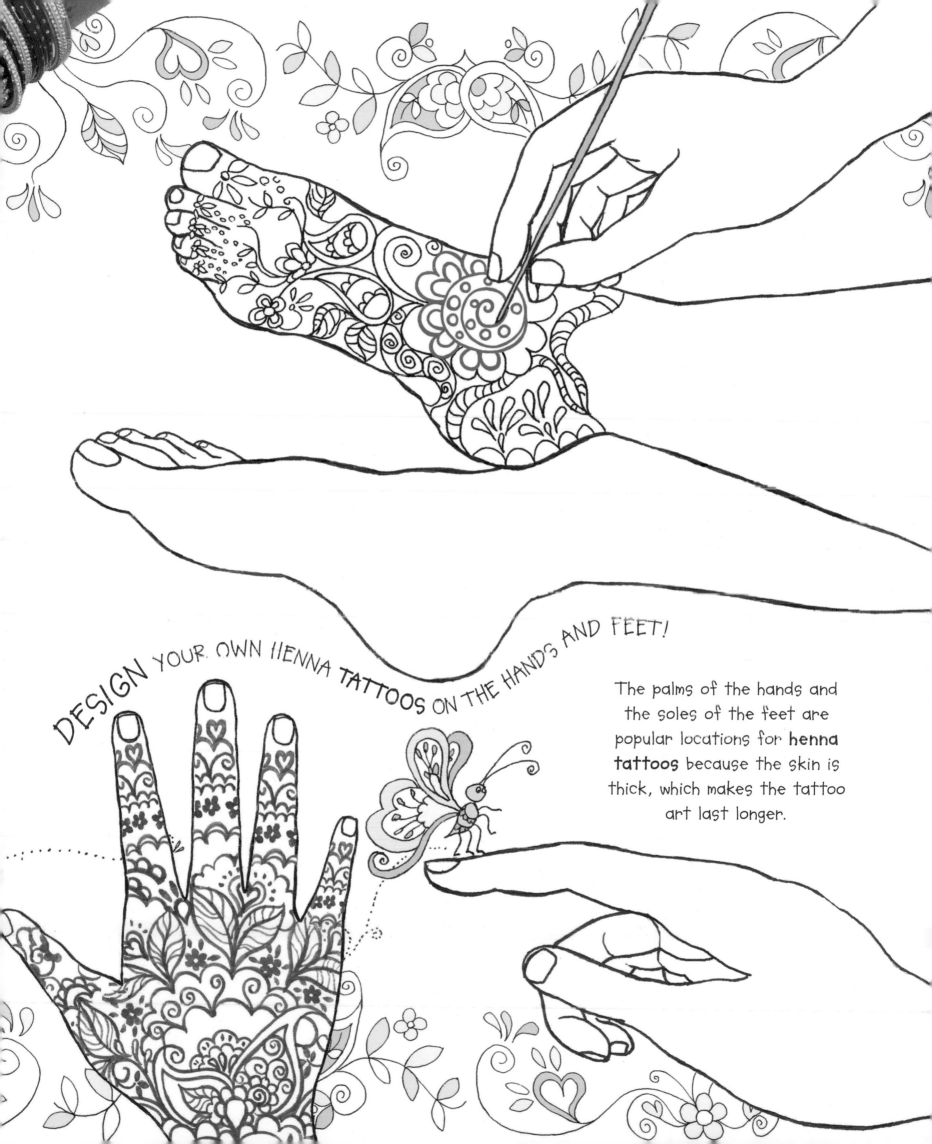

DESIGN YOUR OWN HENNA TATTOOS ON THE HANDS AND FEET!

The palms of the hands and the soles of the feet are popular locations for **henna tattoos** because the skin is thick, which makes the tattoo art last longer.

Lost in a hedgerow!

Have you ever tried to find your way around a **maze**? Mazes are **outdoor puzzles** formed by **high hedges**. There are two types of maze. **Branching mazes** have only one path to the center. **Island mazes** have several. Both are full of **forked paths** and **dead ends**, but you can always find your way to the center and out of a branched maze by keeping your right hand on the wall.

FINISH

START

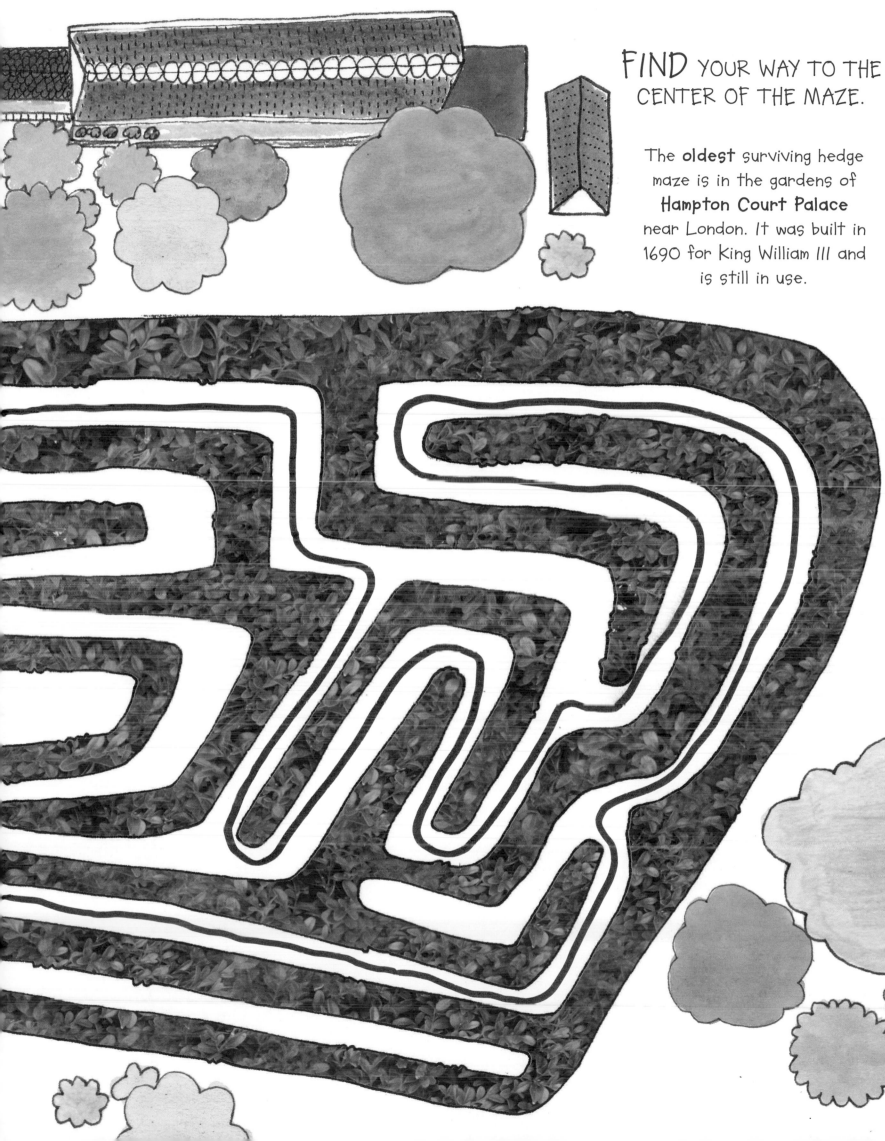

FIND YOUR WAY TO THE CENTER OF THE MAZE.

The **oldest** surviving hedge maze is in the gardens of **Hampton Court Palace** near London. It was built in 1690 for King William III and is still in use.

DRAW MORE BEAUTIFUL BUTTERFLIES.

Butterflies love drinking a flower's nectar. You can **attract** butterflies to your yard by planting plenty of **flowers**, especially ones that are red, yellow, orange, pink, and purple.

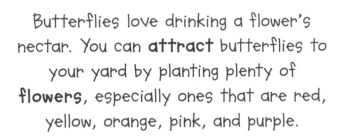

Butterflies can taste with their **feet** as well as their antennae. When they land on a leaf, their feet tell them if it's a good place to **lay their eggs.**

Butterfly garden!

A **butterfly** needs to have plenty to **drink** to keep up its **energy** levels. Most adult butterflies flit between colorful **flowers**, sipping the **nectar** through a strawlike sucker called a **proboscis**, which is coiled under their heads. Butterflies will drink **juice from fruit**, moisture from **wet sand** or **mud**, and even liquid in **animal droppings**! Yuk!

Come inside!

It's lots of fun to open a **doll's house**, arrange the furniture, and invent stories about the people who live there. But the first dolls' houses, produced in Europe in the 16th century, were not toys at all. They were **handmade**, with very detailed furnishings, and were usually replicas of rich peoples' houses. They were so expensive that only very **wealthy** ladies could afford to have one.

DRAW THE BEDROOM.

DRAW THE LIVING ROOM.

Some dolls' house are incredibly **realistic**— they have **lights** and **plumbing** that work and real miniature books in the library.

DRAW THE PLAY ROOM.

DRAW THE KITCHEN.

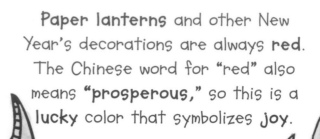

Paper lanterns and other New Year's decorations are always **red**. The Chinese word for "red" also means **"prosperous,"** so this is a **lucky** color that symbolizes **joy**.

All the **colors** used to decorate the dragon have **special meanings**. **Green** symbolizes a **good harvest** and **gold** and **silver** represent **wealth**.

Money is given to children in **red envelopes** at the Chinese New Year.

COLOR IN THE CHINESE DRAGON.

Dancing dragon!

When it's **Chinese New Year**, everyone celebrates with **drums**, **cymbals**, and **dragons**. For Chinese people, dragons are **helpful**, **friendly creatures** who represent **good luck** and **a long life**, so the **dragon dance** is said to chase away **evil spirits**. A dragon can be up to 330 ft (100 m) long and may need **50 dancers** to operate it. The longer the dragon, the luckier it is thought to be.

Shoes! Shoes! Shoes!

Shoes come in many shapes and sizes. Boots, sneakers, sandals, galoshes, flip-flops—the list is nearly endless! But sometimes the most important thing about a shoe is not whether it is **practical** or **comfortable**, but **what it looks like**. Think of the **stiletto heels** that models and movie stars wear for special occasions. You wouldn't be able to run for the bus wearing them—but they look gorgeous!

Some of the most **famous shoes** ever are the **ruby slippers** worn by the actress Judy Garland in *The Wizard of Oz*. Four pairs of them are still in existence, and they are worth around **$2 million each**!

No one really knows why giant pandas are **black and white**, but some scientists think their coloring may help to **camouflage** them among snow and rocks.

Bamboo on the menu!

If you are a **giant panda**, it's essential to like **bamboo**. This **woody plant** is practically all they eat, but luckily they are surrounded by vast forests of bamboo in their home region of central China. Giant pandas are a type of **bear**. They live alone and spend most of their time on the ground, munching—you guessed it—bamboo!

Designer windows!

The ancient craft of **stained glass** is still popular today. To create each intricate design, the artist begins with a **design sketch**. This is divided into shapes according to color. Each piece of glass is cut according to this template and slotted into a **flexible lead strip**. The lead strips are **soldered** (joined) together, an **oily cement** is added to the joins between the glass and the lead to hold the glass securely, and then the whole piece is held in place by a **rigid frame**.

DESIGN YOUR OWN STAINED-GLASS WINDOW.

Hundreds of years ago, when **paper** was very **expensive**, **stained-glass artists** used to paint a **table** white and draw their glass design right onto it!

Anyone want a hug?

The name **"teddy bear"** can be traced back to the early 1900s. It all started in 1902 with a newspaper story about the then US **President Theodore (Teddy) Roosevelt**, who refused to kill a wounded **bear** while on a bear hunt. A cartoon showed the president with the bear, and the phrase "teddy bear" was born. A **stuffed-animal maker** in New York began to use the term "teddy bear" for his toys, and the name stuck.

DRAW YOUR OWN CUDDLY TEDDY BEAR.

Early teddy bears were made to look like **real bears**. Now they're made to look and feel soft and cuddly.

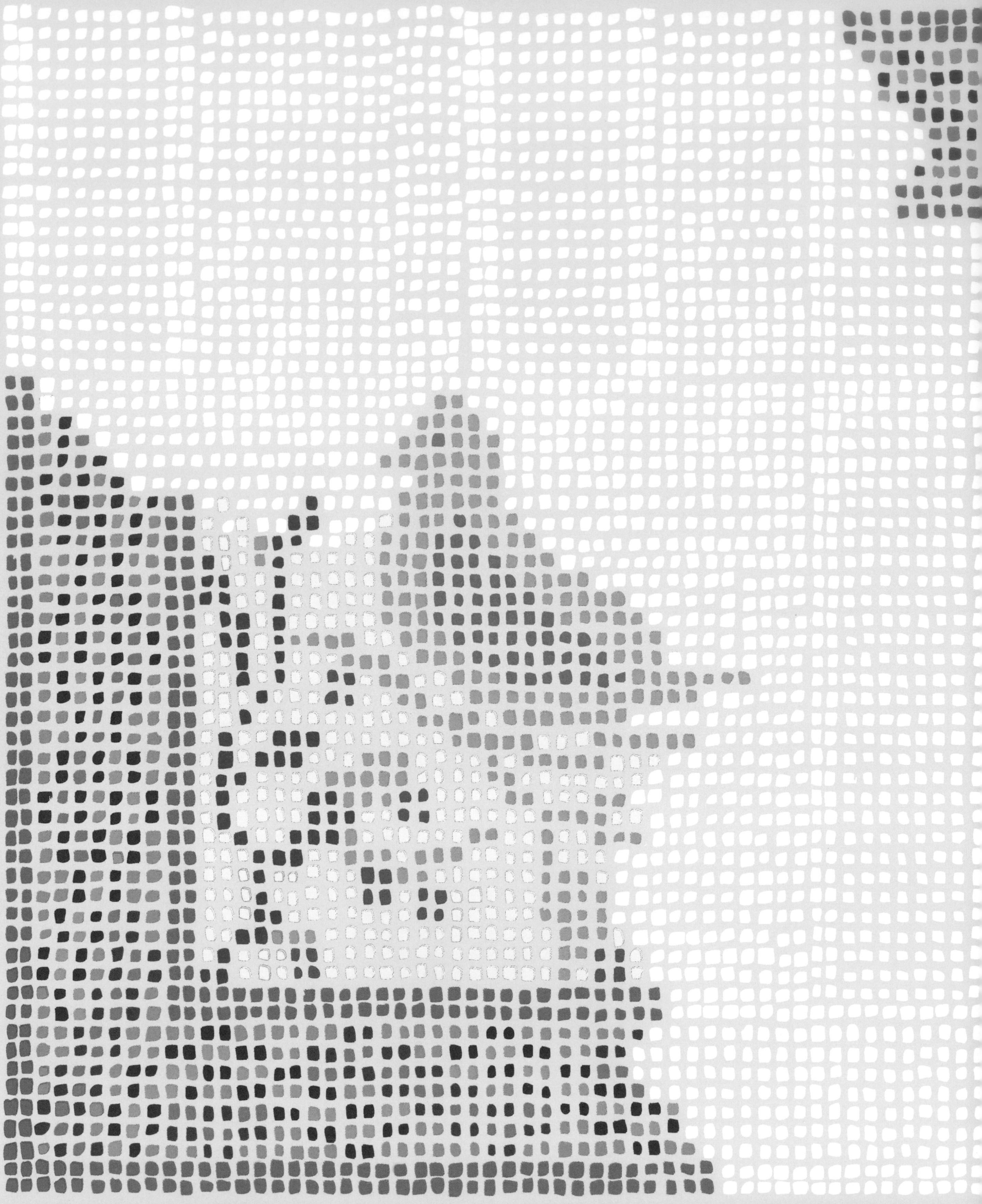

Make a mosaic!

A **mosaic** is a pattern or picture made from **small pieces** of a material, such as **pottery** or **glass**. People have been making mosaics for hundreds of years. They were very fashionable in **Roman times**. Rich people **decorated the floors** of their houses with elaborate mosaic scenes, which would have taken **craftsmen** months to design and lay. It's a little easier for today's **artists**, who make mosaics out of anything—postage stamps, barcodes, sticky notes, even food!

COLOR THE SQUARES
TO COMPLETE THE MOSAIC.

The **world's largest photo mosaic** was created in **Japan** in 2011 with 137,200 **photos**. It measured 16,817.30 sq feet (1,562.39 sq meters)!

Top of the trees!

There are around 10,000 types of **tree** in the world, but most people would have trouble naming more than a dozen. Trees can look very different—their leaves alone can range from tiny needles on **pine trees** to great big **palm leaves**. But all trees share a few vital characteristics: they have just one **stem** (the trunk), they have **branches, leaves,** and **roots,** and they can live for many years.

DRAW MORE TREES TO FILL THE FOREST.

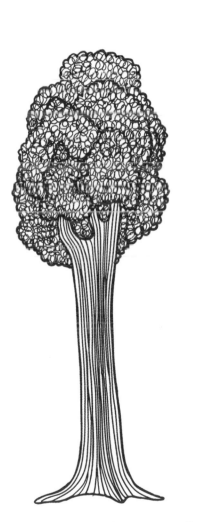

The record-holder for the **tallest tree** is an American **coast redwood** that grew to over 379 ft (115m)— that's almost **27 double-decker buses** stacked on top of each other!

Bubbly cake!

There's a real science to **baking a cake**. When you **stir** a **cake mixture** and bake it, you are actually creating a chemical reaction. **Beating** the ingredients **adds air bubbles**. More **gas bubbles** are created when a **rising agent**, such as self-rising flour or baking soda, is added. All these **bubbles expand when heated**, the mixture hardens, and ding! a yummy cake is ready to eat!

DECORATE THE CAKE WITH BEAUTIFUL DESIGNS.

DRAW MORE DELICIOUS CUPCAKES
TO PUT ON THE STAND.

It is said that if an **unmarried** wedding guest places a piece of wedding cake **under their pillow, they will dream of** their **future love!**

The **fastest** breed of dog is the **greyhound**. Racing greyhounds can reach their top speed of 43 mph (70 kph) in just six strides!

DRAW MORE DOGS HAVING FUN IN THE PARK.

Dogs come in many shapes and sizes, from the massive **Great Dane**, which is about 2ft 7in (80 cm) tall, to the teensy **Chihuahua**, which is only about 8 in (20 cm) high.

Woof, woof!

People have been keeping **dogs** for more than 14,000 years. In fact, dogs were probably the very **first animals to be domesticated**, and it's not hard to see why. Dogs are **hard workers** who can be **trained** to do a huge range of jobs for us—rounding up sheep, sniffing out smuggled goods, guiding blind people, guarding buildings, and much more. And, of course, dogs are our absolute **best friends**. Who else would be so thrilled to see you, every single day?

In fan signals, placing your fan near your heart meant "I love you."

I'm a fan!

Fans have been in use for nearly 3,000 years. They began as a simple way to **keep cool**, but over time they began to be used in **ceremonies** and were even used as a way of **signaling messages** across a room. The **sticks** were often made of **ivory** or **tortoiseshell** and **decorated** with precious **gemstones**. The "leaf" of the fan was made of **paper**, **vellum** (thin animal skin), or **silk**, and **hand-painted** by craftsmen.

DESIGN YOUR OWN FAN PATTERN.

Fan **leaves** were sometimes made of **feathers**, especially **ostrich** or **peacock**.

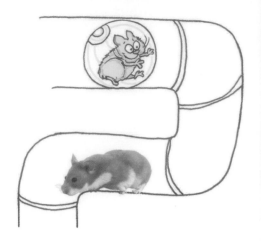

DESIGN THE HAMSTER A NEW HOME AND HELP HIM FIND HIS LUNCH.

Hamsters normally live for two years, although some can live longer!

Happy hamsters!

Hamsters are fantastic pets. These plump little **rodents** are full of personality and are really active little animals. When you own and care for a hamster you have to make sure it has a comfortable, **dry home**, access to **clean water**, and a balanced diet. Hamsters can be very happy living by themselves, and some **don't mix** very well with other hamsters. They also need lots of space to exercise and places to sleep during the day without being disturbed.

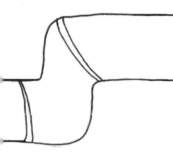

In the wild, hamsters are mainly **nocturnal** animals; this means they are awake and active during the night.

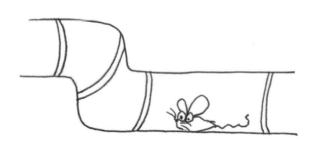

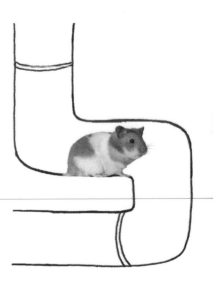

Glass can be formed when a stroke of **lightning** hits sand.

DESIGN YOUR OWN WACKY
GLASS SCULPTURES.

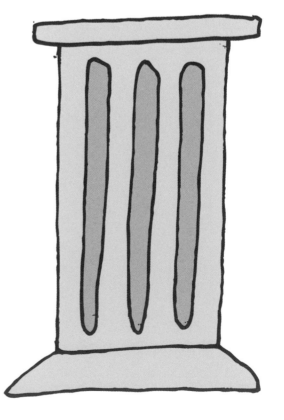

Sandy glass!

Did you know that **glass** is made of **sand**? Sand and other **chemicals** are mixed together, then **heated** to an extremely **high temperature**. The mixture melts and becomes a thick liquid. While it is **cooling** it can be bent into different shapes or poured out flat to make windows and mirrors. **Glass sculptures** can be made by twisting and stretching the glass into all sorts of shapes, and adding other pieces of **colored glass** so that it all sticks together as it cools.

FIND AND COLOR
THE RACCOONS.

COLOR THE MAPLE
LEAVES IN PRETTY
FALL COLORS.

Peekaboo!

Maple trees are found all over the Northern Hemisphere, especially in North America. The large maple leaves turn bright shades of **red** and **gold** in the fall. These forests are full of **wildlife**. One inhabitant is the **raccoon**, a black-and-white **mammal** with a doglike face and a long **bushy tail**. These mischievous animals have a patch of black fur around their eyes that makes them look like masked bandits!

The **largest maple leaf** was found by a boy in Canada. It reached 13 in (36 cm) wide and 11 in (29 cm) in length! That's **three times** as big as your head!

Pots galore!

In **ancient Greece**, ceramic (clay) pots were used for almost everything—eating, drinking, storage, carrying water. The Greeks dug **clay** out of the ground and shaped it by hand. The pot was then fired (baked) in a kiln (a hot oven), to make it **hard and waterproof**. The pots were often produced by **skilled craftsmen** and **painted with scenes** from daily life or **myths** about heroes and gods.

DESIGN YOUR OWN POTS.

Rocket scientists are studying ancient Greek pots to see how the colors **withstand intense heat**. They hope it will help them develop ceramic, heat-resistant tiles for **spacecraft**.

COMPLETE THE DESIGN ON THE POTS.

Sparkly jewels!

Diamonds, sapphires, rubies, and other **jewels** certainly look pretty on a necklace, and because these **stones** are **rare** they are very **valuable,** too. A gemstone has to be carefully cut to **shape** and **polished** before it can be used in a piece of **jewelry**. Each jewel shape has a name, such as "round brilliant," "cabochon," or "princess cut."

DRAW MORE NECKLACES WITH GORGEOUS JEWELS.

One of the world's most **expensive** pieces of jewelry is a **necklace** made for the movie star Elizabeth Taylor. It is made of **diamonds**, **rubies**, and an enormous **pearl** named **"La Peregrina"** and sold for $11.8 million in 2012!

The bigger and more sparkly the stone, the more **expensive** the necklace!

Who are you?

Have you ever been turned into a lion or a butterfly by having your **face painted**? Wearing **makeup** helps an actor's face look **stronger** under the bright **stage lights**, so it can be seen from the back of the theater. **Makeup artists** can completely change how someone looks by adding **pieces of rubber** to give them **wrinkles**, **warts**, or **bulging noses**. Wigs and **false teeth** often complete the look.

Every **clown** has their own **unique** makeup design, which they **register** so that no one else can use it.

DESIGN MAKEUP FACES FOR THESE ACTORS ABOUT TO GO ON STAGE.

The white palace!

The Taj Mahal is an **Indian palace** (Taj Mahal means "Crown Palace") and is built from **white marble**. It took nearly 20,000 workers 16 years to build, and it was finished in 1648. The Taj Mahal's impressive symmetrical architecture amazes millions of visitors every year. It was built by **Shah Jahan** to celebrate the life of his dead wife, Queen Mumtaz Mahal, who is buried there.

The insides of the Taj Mahal are **decorated** with 28 different **precious gems** and **stones**.

The Taj Mahal was made a **World Heritage** site in 1983.

Greetings from India!

FINISH THE TAJ MAHAL.

DRAW MORE DOLPHINS LEAPING INTO THE AIR.

Jumping for joy!

The most **playful** of sea animals, **dolphins** love to **leap** out of the water and **dive** back in. Dolphins are **not fish** but **mammals**, which means they have to come to the surface to **breathe** air. These **intelligent** animals live in small groups and **communicate** by **making clicks** and **whistles**. Like humans, dolphins have their own names and say them when they meet each other.

A **flick** of its **powerful tail** sends the dolphin **soaring** up into the air. Some dolphins do spins or **somersaults** as they leap.

ПОЧТА СССР 16к
1967 ДЕНЬ КОСМОНАВТИКИ

ПОЧТА

The **most expensive** stamp is the **yellow "three skilling"** from **Sweden**. This stamp was **normally green**—the yellow one was a mistake. Only one exists now. It last sold for $2.3 million!

DESIGN YOUR OWN STAMPS FOR THESE LETTERS.

中国人民邮政
T.90.1(1-1)

My stamp collection!

Postage stamps were invented in the UK in the 1840s to show that the **sender** had **paid for a letter** to be sent in the mail. They now come in an amazing range of **shapes** and **sizes** and are illustrated with lots of **different subjects**. This makes stamps ideal things to collect and **rare** stamps can be **extremely valuable**.

8分
庚午年　中国人民邮政
T.146.(1−1)　1990

DRAW AND COLOR MORE BALLOONS.

Up, up, and away!

A **hot-air balloon** may not be the fastest way to travel, but it is probably one of the most amazing! A **burner** under the balloon burns **propane gas**, which **heats the air** inside the balloon. As the air warms up, the balloon **rises**. To go higher, the pilot turns up the **flame**. To stop rising or lose height, he pulls a cord, which opens a **valve** at the top of the balloon and allows some hot air to **escape**.

The **highest** a balloon has ever flown was in 2005 in **Mumbai, India**. It went up 69,852 ft (21,290 meters)—that's 13 miles (21 km) high!

The first **passengers** of the very first hot-air balloon in 1783 were a **sheep**, a **rooster**, and a **duck**!

DESIGN YOUR OWN BALLOON.

Owls everywhere!

Don't let their fluffy **feathers** and cute faces deceive you—**owls** are armed with vicious **beaks** and sharp hooked nails called **talons**. But it's their secret weapons that make them so dangerous—the circle of feathers around their faces **directs sounds** into their ears, giving them **excellent hearing** for locating mice, voles, and other prey. Their **huge eyes** allow them to see at night and they **fly** almost **silently**, so they can **swoop down** on their unsuspecting victims.

Owls **swallow** their prey **whole**, then cough up the bones, fur, and other bits they can't digest in a lump called a **pellet**.

FIND AND COLOR THE OWLS.

An owl's **eyes** can't move in their sockets like ours can, so the bird has to move its head to look in another direction. It can turn its head **all the way around** to see behind it.

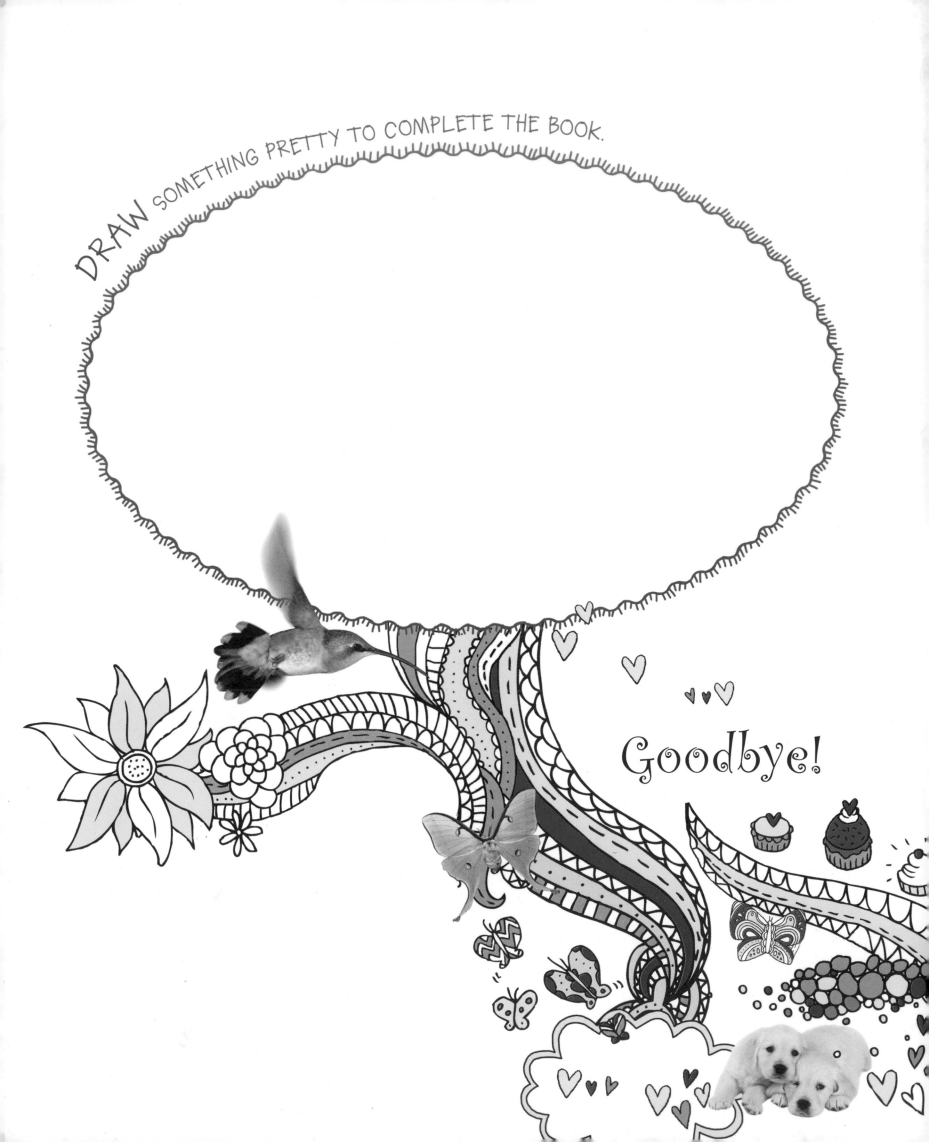